PIANO · VOCAL · GUITAR

AMY GRANT
SOMEWHERE DOWN THE ROAD

W9-BXE-731

CONTENTS

WWW.AMYGRANT.COM

Alfred

Produced by
Alfred Music Publishing Co., Inc.
P.O. Box 10003
Van Nuys, CA 91410-0003
alfred.com

Printed in USA.

ISBN-10: 0-7390-7491-1
ISBN-13: 978-0-7390-7491-6
www.emicmg.com

Front cover painting: Amy Grant; Back cover photo: Kristin Barlowe

 Alfred Cares. Contents printed on 100% recycled paper.

BETTER THAN A HALLELUJAH
CHAPIN HARTFORD AND SARAH HART

"I've loved this song since I first heard it. The honesty and vulnerability of the lyric reminds me that to pray means to come as I am, imperfections and all, because ultimately, God seeks communion with us, the real us...and that's freeing."

God loves a lullaby in a mother's tears in the dead of night · Better than a Hallelujah sometimes · God loves a drunkard's cry, the soldier's plea not to let him die · Better than a Hallelujah sometimes

We pour out our miseries, God just hears a melody · Beautiful the mess we are, the honest cries, of breaking hearts · Are better than a Hallelujah

A woman holding on for life, a dying man giving up the fight · Are better than a Hallelujah sometimes · Tears of shame for what's been done · The silence when the words won't come · Are better than a Hallelujah sometimes ·· Better than a church bell ringing · Better than a choir singing out, singing out

OVERNIGHT (FEATURING SARAH CHAPMAN)
AMY GRANT, NATALIE HEMBY, LUKE LAIRD AND AUDREY SPILLMAN

"I had been trying for some time to find a song to sing with my daughter, Sarah. At 17 and 49, she and I see life from different perspectives. What I appreciate about this song is its simple message: if the good stuff happened 'overnight' you wouldn't understand the value of it. That's true at any age. Besides, the richest experiences in life are often not what we've planned for, but what comes at us sideways when we're least expecting it."

So you've handed in your resignation · Contemplating why nothing turns out right · A little fed up with all the disappointment · So what's the point in wasting any time ·· It's only temporary · So what's your hurry · No need to worry don't you know that

If it all just happened overnight · You wouldn't know how much it means · If it all just happened overnight · You would never learn to believe what you cannot see

I feel like my pace is at a standstill · Do I wait 'till it falls into my hands · A long highway ahead getting started · Steady hearted is what I think I am ·· There's something to be said for experience · Who knows what's ahead keep on going · Take it a day at a time · One foot in front of the other · Take it a day at a time · No need to hurry · Take it a day at a time · It won't happen overnight ·· Have a little faith · You must appreciate every single day · Don't give up no

EVERY ROAD
AMY GRANT AND WAYNE KIRKPATRICK

"No experience in life is wasted. Everything we go through provides us a unique opportunity to know ourselves and to know God."

There you go making mountains · Out of such a little hill · Here I go mixing mortar · For another wall to build · There's a struggle in this life we lead · It's partly you · It's partly me (but)

Every road that's traveled · Teaches something new · And every road that's narrow · Pushes us to choose · And I'd be lying if I said · I had not tried to leave a time or two · But every road that leads me · Leads me back to you

Here we stand in the middle · Of what we've come to know · It's a dance, it's a balance · Holding on and letting go · But there is nothing that we can't resolve · When love's at stake · When love's involved

UNAFRAID
AMY GRANT AND WAYNE KIRKPATRICK

"Songwriting is a form of contemplation. To write about someone or something, you have to meditate on that person or that idea until the swirl of feelings surrounding it can be expressed in words. The process is worthwhile, whether or not you end up writing a song. I wept a bucket of gratitude writing this one."

Woke up this morning with you in our bed · Going over and over everything you said · Who taught you how to speak the words that you say · I've always wanted to be talked to that way

·· **Love has made · Has made you unafraid** ··

Watching my children finding their way · Through struggles and triumphs and heartbreak · I hope the roads they take are making them strong · I'll still be on my knees long after they're gone

·· **Love has made · Love has made · Love has made · Has made me unafraid** ··

My lovely mother is getting on in years · And the way her body's aging brings her girls to tears · The way she trembles with each effort she makes · She just says heaven's getting closer each day

·· **'Cause love has made · Love has made · Love has made · Has made her unafraid ·· Love could make · Love can make · Love will make · Make you unafraid**

HARD TIMES

AMY GRANT, IAN FITCHUK AND JUSTIN LOUCKS

"How quickly the time goes by. How quickly the torch is passed from one generation to the next. I'm grateful for the sheltering love of the older generations of my family. They are almost all gone now, but I learned what I needed to know from them."

I smile when I remember all the things we did · The worlds we discovered when I was a kid · Sitting on your shoulders I was riding high · All of life before me, I could see for miles ·· You gave me a life to love · Showed me the dreams I was dreaming of · Told me love was enough

Then hard times come · Hard times come · Hard times come for everyone · Hard times come · Hard times come · And they'll come 'till we're done

Lately I've been standing on my own two feet · There's a pair of watchful eyes staring up at me · I will turn them toward the sunrise · Turn them toward the stars · Where the beauty of a new day will always fill the heart ·· Give you a life to love · Show you dreams you're dreaming of · Just let love be enough ·· Making you measure what you're made of · Helping you galvanize the love

Cause hard times come, they come · Hard times come to everyone · Hard times come · Hard times come · And they'll come 'till we're done

WHAT IS THE CHANCE OF THAT

AMY GRANT AND WAYNE KIRKPATRICK

I wrote this song in 1996. I was asking a lot of questions about truth and reality in those last couple of years of my first marriage. With so much uncertainty in my life, music was a safe place to explore the landscape. A lot has changed since then. …I still like trains."

Tonight I've been counting railroad cars · Clinking and grinding into the dark · One of them passed with an open door · And I pictured myself jumping on board · What is the chance of that ·· Well I've always had this thing about trains · A lonesome sound like a man in pain · Going somewhere they don't lose track · Some folks leave and they don't look back · What is the chance of that

I have believed since I was a little bitty girl · That there were rules of cause and effect · And they slowly shaped my world · But pain and hard times they come and they go · Like some blindfolded angel somewhere saying · Eeny Meeny Miny Moe · What is the chance of that ··

Why do I feel restless inside · Maybe I'm part of a wandering tribe · I want to check my family tree · I think there's a little nomad in me · What is the chance of that ·· Life is a thing you drink in deep · The journey is hard and the journey's sweet · Maybe I'll search and maybe I'll find · Things I wanted were already mine · What is the chance of that

I have believed since I was a little bitty girl · That there were rules of cause and effect · And they slowly shaped my world · But pain and hard times they come and they go · Like some test of faith that purifies my · Weak belief into something gold · What is the chance of that

SOMEWHERE DOWN THE ROAD

AMY GRANT AND WAYNE KIRKPATRICK

"I wrote this chorus on a chilly night spent in an old gutted-out cabin, under an April full moon in 1995. The children were finally asleep. A good friend and I were settling into another conversation about the 'why's' in life. The song just slipped out."

So much pain and no good reason why · You've cried until the tears run dry · And nothing here can make you understand · The one thing that you held so dear · Is slipping from your hands · And you say ·· Why, why, why · Does it go this way · Why, why, why · And all I can say is

·· Somewhere down the road · There'll be answers to the questions · Somewhere down the road · Though we cannot see it now · Somewhere down the road · You will find mighty arms reaching for you · And they will hold the answers at the end of the road ··

Yesterday I thought I'd seen it all · I thought I'd climbed the highest wall · Now I see the learning never ends · And all I know to do is keep on walking · Walking 'round the bend, saying ·· Why, why, why · Does it go this way · Why, why, why · And all I can say is · All I know to say now

THIRD WORLD WOMAN

AMY GRANT AND CHRIS EATON

"Do unto others as you would have them do unto you."

What if I were that mother staring from my TV · What if that were my brown-eyed baby · Hungry as she could be · What if that were my family · What if that was my world · Waiting on water waiting on a vaccine · Waiting on someone to bring me a bag of beans

Lord have mercy on me

What if I was that mother and I was waiting on me · The big success so well dressed on the other side of the sea · Living with my distractions · Life's been good to me · Maybe she's praying · Praying for a miracle · Maybe the answer is me ·· Lord have mercy on me

I was born in Georgia where I could do as I pleased · And I can get my hands on just about anything I might need · Who's that third world woman maybe she could be · Could be mother could be daughter could be sister to me ·· Lord have mercy on me

FIND WHAT YOU'RE LOOKING FOR
Amy Grant and Mindy Smith

"The inspiration for this song came from Mary Elizabeth Chapman, grandmother of my three older children, Matt, Millie and Sarah. She was full of homespun wisdom, and spoke these words to me often. 'There's a little good in the worst of us, and a little bad in the best of us, so it never behooves any of us to criticize the rest of us.' (Always said with a smile.) I built the song around it to remember her."

What would they find if they uncovered all of my tracks · Of roads I'd snuck down and darkness and never turn back · Well they'd find what they're looking for · Secrets and so much more ·· What would they find if they searched for a heart of gold · They'd find sacrifices of time and of money never told · Yeah they'd find what they're looking for · Kindness and so much more

Cause there's so much good in the worst of us · So much bad in the best of us · It never makes sense for any of us · To criticize the rest of us · We'll just find what we're looking for · We'll find it and so much more

What would I find if I turned back the time on your face · Could I piece together the memories that have made you this way · I might find what I'm looking for · Understanding and so much more ·· Haven't we all learned the best life lessons · By falling, and falling down hard · If we're looking for somebody's failures · We won't have to look very far

COME INTO MY WORLD
Amy Grant

"I included this 1996 recording because it is so raw and was so true at the time. Pain isolates us. Nobody knows when you're smiling on the outside and dying on the inside: except the one who stands at the door and knocks."

Come into my world · Come crashing through the ceiling · And find the messy rooms, the scattered pearls · If you are brave then come into my world

Come into my world · So lovely from the outside · So dark in here the demons dance and twirl · And find their pleasure frightening this girl · If you are brave then come into my world

Cause I never saw the changes come · Or knew enough to run when this old house had come undone · And now I'm buried in the walls · And no one comes to call but you · Come into my world

Come into my world · I can not find the doorway · It's overgrown with vines that twist and curl · If you are brave then come into my world

Come into my world · There'll be no other invitation · Not another sound another word · Nothing more than you've already heard · Please be brave and come into my world

ARMS OF LOVE (2010 version)
Amy Grant, Michael W. Smith, and Gary Chapman

"It's been almost 30 years since I first sang Arms of Love. What a treat to rerecord it in my 50th year...a little lower, a little slower. Ha! And still true."

Lord, I'm really glad You're here · I hope You feel the same when You see all my fear · And how I fail ·· I fall sometimes · It's hard to walk in shifting sand · I miss the rock and find I've nowhere left to stand · I start to cry · Please help me raise my hand so You can pick me up · Hold me close · Hold me tighter

·· I have found a place where I can hide · It's safe inside · Your arms of love · Like a child who's held throughout a storm · You keep me warm · In Your arms of love ··

Storms will come and storms will go · I wonder just how many storms it takes until I finally know · You're here always · Even when my skies are far from gray · I can stay · Teach me to stay there

IMAGINE / SING THE WONDROUS LOVE OF JESUS
Amy Grant, Bart Millard, Eliza E. Hewitt and Emily D. Wilson
Arranged by Vince Gill and Brown Bannister

"Nobody gets out of here alive, but I trust that the best part of the journey will be waiting on the other side."

I can only imagine what it will be like · When I walk by Your side · I can only imagine what my eyes will see · When Your face is looking at me · Surrounded by Your glory what will my heart feel · Will I dance for You Jesus or in awe of You be still · Imagine, I can only imagine ··

I can only imagine all creation bowed down · The whole universe saying Your name out loud · I can only imagine all our broken lives · Resurrected in the healing light ·

Surrounded by Your glory what will my heart feel · Will I dance for You Jesus or in awe of You be still · Will I stand in Your presence or to my knees will I fall · Will I sing Hallelujah, will I be able to speak at all · I can only imagine, I can only imagine ··

Surrounded by forgiveness, what will my heart feel · Will I dance for You Jesus or in awe of You be still · Will I stand in Your presence or to my knees will I fall · Will I sing Hallelujah, will I be able to speak at all ·

I can only imagine, oh I can only imagine · I can only imagine, oh I can only imagine · I can only imagine, just imagine · I can only imagine, imagine ·

Sing the wondrous love of Jesus · Sing His mercy and His grace · In the mansions bright and blessed · He'll prepare for us a place

OVERNIGHT

Words and Music by
AMY GRANT, NATALIE HEMBY, LUKE LAIRD
and AUDREY SPILLMAN

*Play cue notes 2nd time only.

Overnight - 7 - 1

8

Chorus:

BETTER THAN A HALLELUJAH

Words and Music by
CHAPIN HARTFORD and SARAH HART

Moderately ♩ = 76

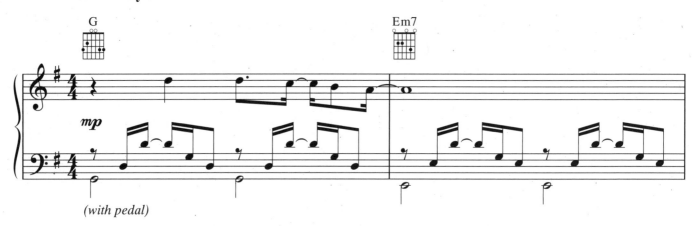

(with pedal)

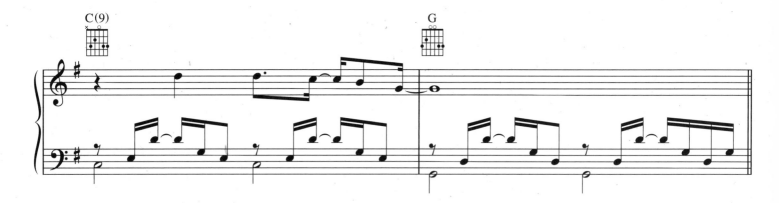

Verse 1 (sing 1st time only):

1. God loves a lul-la-by in a moth-er's tears in the dead of night

Verse 2 (sing 2nd time only):

2. The wom-an hold-ing on for life, a dy-ing man giv-ing up the fight are

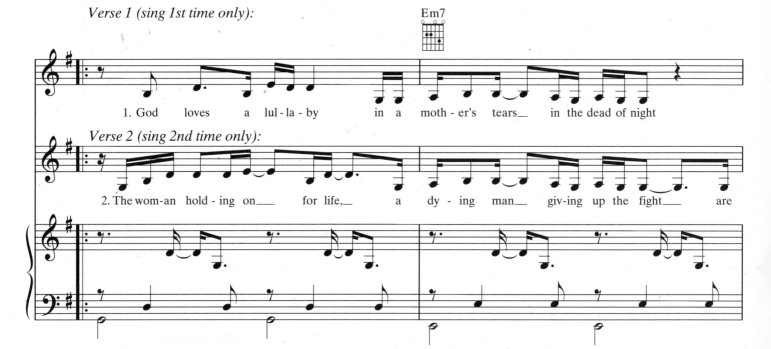

Better Than a Hallelujah - 6 - 1

14 *Chorus:*

EVERY ROAD

Words and Music by
AMY GRANT and WAYNE KIRKPATRICK

Moderately ♩ = 120

Now, I'd be ly - ing if I said_____ I had not tried_

_ to leave_ a time_ or two.__ But ev - 'ry road_ that leads_

_ me,___ leads me back_ to you.____

2. Here we

Verse 2:

UNAFRAID

Words and Music by
AMY GRANT and WAYNE KIRKPATRICK

Moderately slow ♩ = 84   *Verse 1:*

1. Woke up___ this morn-ing with

you in our___ bed,___ go-ing o-ver and___ o-ver ev-'ry-thing you said.___

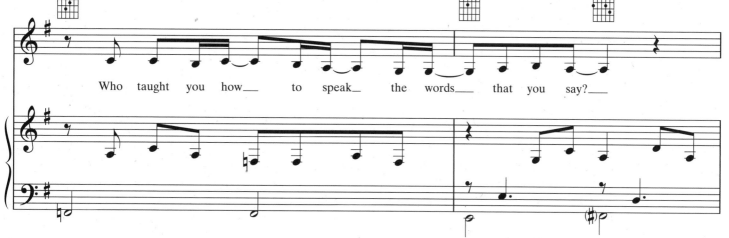

Who taught you how___ to speak___ the words___ that you say?___

Unafraid - 5 - 1

HARD TIMES

Words and Music by
AMY GRANT, IAN FITCHUK
and JUSTIN LOUCKS

Hard Times - 5 - 1

Chorus:

WHAT IS THE CHANCE OF THAT

Words and Music by
AMY GRANT and WAYNE KIRKPATRICK

Moderately slow ♩ = 84

Verse:

1. To - night, I've been count - ing rail - road cars,
2. Why do I feel rest - less in - side?

clink-ing and grind - ing in - to the dark. One of them passed with an o - pen door, and I
May - be I'm part of a wan - der - ing tribe. I want to check my fam - i - ly tree, I

pic - tured my - self jump-ing on board. What is the chance of that?
think there's a lit - tle no - mad in *me.* What is the chance of that?

What Is the Chance of That - 5 - 1

SOMEWHERE DOWN THE ROAD

Slowly ♩ = 69

Words and Music by
AMY GRANT and WAYNE KIRKPATRICK

Verse 1:

1. So much pain and no good rea - son why. You've cried un - til the tears run dry. Noth - ing here can make you un - der - stand. The

*Recorded in B major.

Somewhere Down the Road - 9 - 1

Chorus:

44

Chorus:

end   of   the   road._____

Oh,   keep on____ walk-ing, now.

Pre-chorus:

Why, why,_ why_____   does it go____ this way?_   And

THIRD WORLD WOMAN

Words and Music by
AMY GRANT and CHRIS EATON

Moderately slow, with a strong beat ♩ = 76

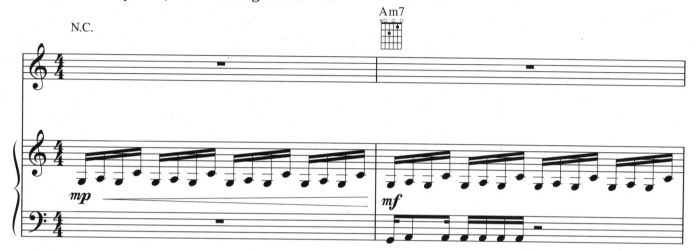

Verse 1:

Third World Woman - 7 - 1

50

Third World Woman - 7 - 2

54

Lord, have mer - cy on___ me.

decresc.

p

FIND WHAT YOU'RE LOOKING FOR

Slowly, with movement, in one ♩. = 52

Words and Music by
AMY GRANT and MINDY SMITH

(with pedal)

Find What You're Looking For - 9 - 1

Verse 1:

1. What would they___ find_____ if they___ un - cov - ered___ all_____ of my_____

___ tracks,___ of roads I'd snuck

down_____ and dark - ness and nev - er turn_____ back?___

Well, they'd_ find_____ what they're_____ look-in'____ for;_

58

%. *Chorus:*

so much good in the worst___ of us, so much___

bad in___ the best of us._____ It nev-er makes___ sense___ for

an-y of us_____ to crit-i-cize___ the rest___

___ of us. We'll just___ find___ what we're_____ look-in'___ for.

To Coda ⊕

Bridge:

64

COME INTO MY WORLD

Words and Music by
AMY GRANT

Moderately ♩ = 84

Verse:

1. Come in-to___ my world.___ Come
2. Come in-to___ my world.___

Come
I

Come Into My World - 5 - 1

68

IMAGINE / SING THE
WONDROUS LOVE OF JESUS

Imagine
Words and Music by
AMY GRANT and BART MILLARD

Sing the Wondrous Love of Jesus
Words by ELIZA E. HEWITT
Music by EMILY D. WILSON
Arranged by VINCE GILL and BROWN BANNISTER

Imagine / Sing the Wondrous Love of Jesus - 8 - 1

72

74

ARMS OF LOVE
(2010 Version)

Words and Music by
AMY GRANT, MICHAEL W. SMITH
and GARY CHAPMAN

Slowly, with expression ♩ = 69

Verse 1:

2. It's hard to walk__ in shift - ing sand.__
3. Storms will come__ and storms__ will go.__

I miss the rock__ and find__ I've no - where left to stand,__ and start__
I won - der just__ how man - y storms__ it takes__ un - til I fi -

__ to cry.__ Please help me raise my hands,__ so You__ can pick__ me
n'lly know__ You're here al - ways. E - ven when__ my skies__ are far__ from

up. Hold me close, hold me__ tight - er.
gray, I can stay, teach me to stay there

* Vocal harmony 3rd verse only.

Arms of Love - 3 - 2

Chorus:

I have found_ a place_ where I____ can hide,
in the place_ I found_ where I____ can hide, } it's safe__ in-

side Your arms_ of love. Like a child_ who's held_ through-out a

storm, You keep_me warm__ in your arms_ of love. love. You keep me

warm__ in your arms_ of love.

a tempo

molto rit.